I0830245

2428 Southmore

Houston, Texas 77004

832-944-2372

Taharka looks on as youth lead demonstration over African Burial Ground in Sugar Land, Texas 2018

THE BLACK UNITY GUIDE

The Operational Unity Network:

Guide for Functional & Practical Unity in the Black Community

By Kofi Taharka

Foreword by Sundiata Acoli, Political Prisoner

Afterword by Folade Madzimoyo

A Black Guerrilla Media Publication

© 2017 Kofi Taharka

All Rights Reserved

ISBN: 9781726628280

KOFI TAHARKA was born and raised in South East Banneker City (Washington, D.C.) His large family instilled in him a sense of Black Pride and devotion of service to his community. While a student in Atlanta, Georgia, Kofi got the opportunity to be exposed to outstanding nationalists, theologians, revolutionaries, Pan-Africanist and African-centered historians.

In the early 1990's in his current home Houston, Texas, Taharka designed and facilitated a functional Operational Unity (OU) Network after hearing the concept in a speech. OU has made profound strides and significant achievements in building a base for unity among African/Black people. In fact, it has been heralded nationally as a practical, functional model for the ever-elusive unity which is often talked about but rarely implemented.

Taharka also has the privilege, honor, and responsibility of being the National Chairman of The National Black United Front (NBUF).

Contents

Foreword

This short powerful piece, A BLACK UNITY GUIDE – the Operational Unity Network (OU), by Kofi Taharka, is about achieving unity without uniformity. In 1993, Kofi organized different groups composed of the National Black United Front (NBUF), the Nation Of Islam Muhammad Mosque #45 (NOI), S.H.A.P.E. Community Center, Ta-seti African Historical Society, Haitian American Ministries (HAM), and The Shrine of the Black Madonna into just such a unified collective.

In 1993, I was at US Penitentiary Leavenworth, Kansas, in my 20th year of imprisonment and in dire need of outside supporters for my ongoing parole process. Kofi stepped up like a friend indeed. He, the NBUF, the NOI and others in his collective and still others in society at large, all provided massive support to my parole effort.

Kofi has been there for me ever since, as well as others from those days. He's my brother, comrade, and friend; also, my "semi-homie." He's from Banneker City (Washington D.C.), but has spent close to 30 years organizing in Houston, Texas. I am from Decatur, Texas. Enjoy his book, he speaks from experience: the best teacher.

- Sundiata Acoli, Political Prisoner (Trenton State Prison, NJ)

Dedication and Challenge

I would like to dedicate this work to the masses of Black/African people who are catching hell fighting on every front from across the globe. It is my hope that in a practical, functional way, this work can help us elevate our condition. In addition, I want to dedicate this writing to my wife Adepeju Oluyemisi and my sons, Kamua Kwesi and Kalomo Yao. They have stuck with me like soldiers and paid a high cost for me to serve my people unbent and unbowed.

Kamua Kwesi, Adepeju Oluyemisi, Kofi Taharka, Kalomo Yao (2000)

Lastly, I want to straight ahead challenge those in high positions of service ("leadership") in the neighborhoods, in the streets and on a national and international level to take a hard look at our condition. Then, drop your egos and petty differences and come together in true "unity" for the good of the whole. Cameo, photo-op unity will not meet the challenges we face, lest the people rise up and move you out of the way.

Introduction

The story I am about to share with you is something that I participated in that is sorely needed in our communities across the world called **Operational Unity** (OU). Throughout this brief pamphlet understand when I use the term "I" it literally means my family, organization, community, elders, youth, and ancestors. One day in the early 1990's, I was driving in my car and listening to a cassette tape. I believe the topic was organizing. The speaker mentioned this concept of Operational Unity.

I am sure this term Operational Unity gained popularity in the Black Power movement of the 1960's. However, as with most ideas, the struggle for African people/Black people to come together goes deep into our past on the continent of Africa and has been consistently apart of our dialogue since suffering the greatest humanity disbursement - the MAAFA (Great Tragedy; otherwise called the European slave trade).

Operational Unity is when groups can work together in a functional way for the upliftment of the whole (African People/Black People) without forfeiting their specific identity, aims or objectives. So, as I was riding in my car and listening, I got to thinking about how Operational Unity could be implemented in the Black community in Houston, Texas. I wanted to take it out of the realm of theory and put it into practice.

8 Unity Steps

1. **INTEGRITY** – If you are organizing for unity make sure you have true motives and principles.
2. **VISUALIZE** – Whether it is street organizations, economic collectives, church or movement formations, for these 8 principles to apply you must be able to see in your mind what you want to happen.
3. **STEPS** – Take the vision and break it down to tangible steps to get you to the final outcome and be flexible enough to adapt the plan.
4. **STUDY** – Know the history and foundation, beliefs etc. of those you are seeking to bring together.
5. **HUMILITY** – Meditate, pray or whatever gets you centered to be humble but assertive to go out and accomplish the vision.
6. **ACTION** – Make the power move; roll out to put the plan into action by following the steps.
7. **PATIENCE** – Exhibit a high degree of patience and undying love for Black/African people.
8. **CRITIQUE** – At every point, be open to constructive criticism and collective input into the process.

Foundation

As I thought about it more and more, and bounced the idea off of a few activists, I began to develop a concept as to how we could make this work in Houston. The first principle that I thought through was which groups could/would/should come together. I was already a member of the National Black United Front-Houston Chapter (NBUF) and had been in the Ta-seti African Historical Society (Study Group), so naturally these groups came to mind.

It was my premise that groups with a similar outlook would be more likely to come together than organizations with radically different approaches to our challenges as a community. In other words, it seemed illogical to me to try and bring together somebody who was trying to cuddle up to the white power structure and a group that was trying to overturn the white power structure, even though they were both African/Black.

The groups I thought had generally similar perspectives were the National Black United Front- Houston Chapter (NBUF), the Ta-seti African Historical Society, The Shrine of the Black Madonna Pan African Orthodox Christian Church (PAOCC), the Nation of Islam Muhammad Mosque #45 (NOI), S.H.A.P.E. Community Center, and later Haitian American Ministries (HAM).

 I had studied the history of all of these groups, participated in some of their activities and to different extents, knew the leadership. Furthermore, I had done some work in the community and possessed a high degree of integrity. This is an important point because I didn't just pop up on the scene and say we need unity, I had a track record.

Next, I developed a three or four-page presentation to make to each group. The foundation of The Operational Unity Network would be simple: each participating group would get to identify 3 events/actions/programs which they could designate as 1. Code Red 2. Code Black 3. Code Green in a one-year period.

At a code red event/action or program all other groups were obligated to promote, attend and support it as if it were their own activity. Code black and code green events required incrementally less support. Also included in the verbal presentations were points from the mission statement, leaflets, and books of the various organizations which stressed the power of unity. The foundation was something simple, functional, benefiting everyone and backed up by a part of the theory of each group.

ENHANCED COMMUNICATION

- Event communication can be handled by a facilitator for the first year.
- Notification of programs must be done <u>3</u> weeks before an event date via telephone and written communication
- Program classification:

CODE

RED

* A code red program will be the one program a organization chooses for maximum support from all other organizations.	* Operational unity commitment under code re includes: announcement of program to you organization, physical attendance at progran by strong contingent of your organization. Support this event as if it were your own organization sponsoring it.

BLACK

* A code black program will be one program a organization chooses for major support from all other organizations.	* Operational unity commitment under code blac includes: announcment of program to your organization and encourage attendance by you membership.

GREEN

* A code green program will be all events sponsored by each organization which the sponsoring organization wishes to communicate.	* Operational unity commitment under code gree includes: whatever support your organizatio can give to the program.

Commitments to Code Red Events

Study/"Know Your People"

"Organize, organize, organize!" - Kwame Ture

Kwame Ture once stated something along the lines of, *if you are serious about organizing in our communities, you must know the history, structure, and political line of other organizations operating in our community.* In coordinating the operational unity process, I took this mandate from our great ancestor Brother Kwame very seriously. It is very beneficial to know and understand the mindset, foundation, history, and beliefs of different formations in our communities in general and specifically when attempting to forge practical unity.

It is no different on the streets knowing the terrain when you are crossing into whose territory, what beefs exist, who's down with who, etc. The principle of knowing your people, knowing your customer, having already thought of the objection before it is made is easily applicable to any sphere in our community. It is called being prepared or knowing your sh**. As was stated earlier, this information can be gained from verbal conversation, leaflets, books, videos, articles, etc.

OPERATIONAL UNITY

GOAL - Organizations of like mind coming together in order to better the condition people of African descent in Houston, Texas.

Making Unity Happen

Taking the three to four-page paper armed with decent knowledge of each group, I went separately to each organization leader and made the presentation. The concept was generally well received and good feedback was taken into account.

I firmly believe one of the many reasons why these representatives responded positively was my age, I was in my early twenties. I say this because of some comments I received in these initial meetings. They were encouraging, yet, skeptical, viewing my youthful naivete about how we could come together in this grand plan of unity. They felt obligated not to kill my young warrior spirit.

After the initial meetings, a series of meetings were held at different locations of the entire group. After going through proper organizational protocol, each group agreed to work together based on the outline and signed a statement to that effect.

OPERATIONAL UNITY

I ___Lorenza "Jelani" Williams___ am a representative of the ___TA-SETI African Historical Society___ have the power and will implement the commitment to operational unity as outlined and agreed upon by participating organizations.

Signature _________________________

Date _____2/13/93_____

Copy of one of the signed agreements

There was excitement among the representatives and it was suggested we should make a big announcement about our unity pack publicly. However, Sister Ada Edwards advised the group not to make a public announcement until we had actually worked together on our first code red activity. Her reasoning was that we should not talk about something we hadn't done yet. When we did make the announcement, we could point back to something we had accomplished, not talking about what we were gonna do, which so many times has failed our people. Her suggestion was accepted.

To me, this was an important and wise move. Significant work took place to get to this point; presentations meetings, phone calls, and more was to come. It was agreed that monthly meetings take place. Out of this Operational Unity, retreats were held to further solidify our foundation.

Sis. Ada Edwards

Getting Over Our Differences

It should be stated that different issues confronted the Operational Unity Network which threatened to derail the process. Some participants had real problems with each other based on confrontations in the past.

Despite the commitment of the representatives to their organizations, sometimes the same commitment did not exist to the network. Missed meetings and late arrivals tested my resolve. At times, I felt like I was babysitting my elders with repeated phone calls and chiding to get them to follow all the way through with the commitment.

Some of this attributed to their hectic schedules, most of these people had major responsibilities in running their own organizations. Therefore, it was important to make the meetings concise and worthy of people's time. From time to time, issues arose regarding different positions different groups took on topics concerning our people. Remember, many of these groups were apart of national organizations and/or had national affiliations.

For the most part these obstacles were able to be overcome with persistence, recognizing the bigger picture and delivering on something of value. As coordinator, many times I had and still have issues with some of the participants positions, politics, etc., but the similarities outweighed the differences.

M E M O R A N D U M

went to all participants

TO: Jelani Williams   DATE: 2/5/93

FROM: Rodney S. Penn

SUBJECT: Operational Unity Meeting

The purpose of this communication is to provide details
concerning the initial meeting of prospective participants
in Operational Unity. The meeting is scheduled for Saturday
February 13th 1993, 12 noon at Shape Community Center (Almeda
location). The meeting agenda will include the following
points of discussion;

    1. Review of Operational Unity concept (if necessary).

    2. Suggestions for enhancements of program.

    3. Equity in financial requirements for code Red events.

    4. Discussion of a type of event which a particular
        organization could not support.

    5. Proposed implementation of program 3/1/93-3/1/94 or
        3/1/93-6/1/94.

    6. Dates for code Red events for each organization.

    7. Signing of commitment.

Enclosed you will find a copy of the Operational Unity
presentation which I made to you a few weeks ago, along
with a copy of the commitment form. Your presence is

The Power of Unity

The ball got rolling in July of 1993 with the first Operational Unity Network Code Red event which was the National Black United Front (NBUF) National Convention held in Houston, Texas. It was merely a coincidence that NBUF, the organization I was a part of, had the first Code Red activity. This was the non-publicized activity which was mentioned earlier.

Participation from other groups focused on workshop facilitation and attendance. The first publicized Code Red event was the S.H.A.P.E. Community Center's annual Unity Fun Run & Walk in the neighborhood. This included cross promotion on radio, leaflets, and television. Members of other groups would go on the radio and promote the Code Red activity of the other organization.

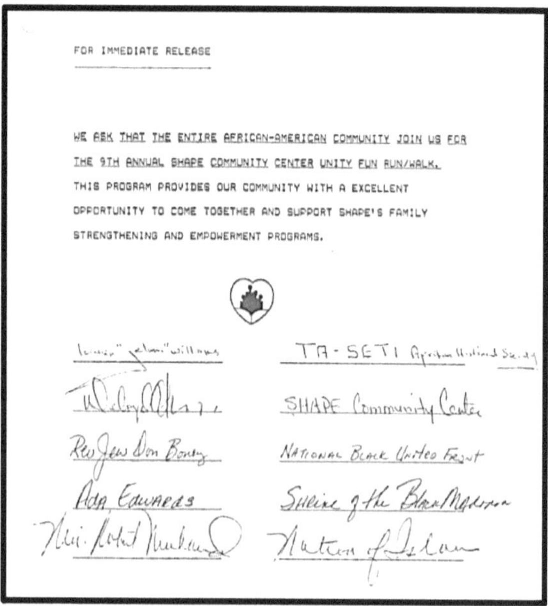

FOR IMMEDIATE RELEASE

WE ASK THAT THE ENTIRE AFRICAN-AMERICAN COMMUNITY JOIN US FOR THE 9TH ANNUAL SHAPE COMMUNITY CENTER UNITY FUN RUN/WALK. THIS PROGRAM PROVIDES OUR COMMUNITY WITH A EXCELLENT OPPORTUNITY TO COME TOGETHER AND SUPPORT SHAPE'S FAMILY STRENGTHENING AND EMPOWERMENT PROGRAMS.

Some Successful OU events:

Haiti/Rwanda Relief Day, 1994

Citywide Radiothon

Raised $20,000.00 and 40,000 tons of food, medical supplies

Houston Delegation Sent to Rwanda

Representatives Took Supplies to Rwanda

Representatives Took Supplies to Haiti

Volunteers from OU set up drop off sites throughout the city

Mawiyah Buseje, Founder of Haitian American Ministries

BOARD OF DIRECTORS

Chairman:
DONALD F. McHENRY
Unversity Research Professor of Diplomacy and
International Affairs, Georgetown University
    er U.S. Permanent Rep. to the U.N.

..e Chair:
AMBASSADOR
OUMAROU G. YOUSSOUFOU

Vice Chair:
DOREEN F. TILGHMAN
Assistant General Secretary,
General Board of Global Ministries,
United Methodist Church

Treasurer:
CLYDE B. RICHARDSON
President, Loriche Productions

Secretary:
JOSEPH C. KENNEDY, Ph.D.
Senior Vice President, Africare

ROBERT S. BROWNE
Economist

CECIL CALLAHAN
Senior Portfolio Manager, INVESCO

GEORGE A. DALLEY, Esq.
Partner, Holland & Knight

MARION M. DAWSON
President, Dearfield Associates

THOMAS DRAPER
President, ComRel, Inc.

JOHN W. ENGLISH
Private Investor

WALTER E. FAUNTROY
President, Walter E. Fauntroy & Associates

NANCY M. FOLGER
Director, Special Projects
   dren's Defense Fund

.NEST G. GREEN
Managing Director, Lehman Brothers

JAMES M. HARKLESS, Esq.
Labor Arbitrator

LEO I. HIGDON, JR.
Dean, Darden School of Business,
University of Virginia

JEROME JACOBSON
President, Economic Studies, Inc.

JAMES JOSEPH
President , Council on Foundations

WILLIAM KIRKER, M.D.

DELANO E. LEWIS, Esq.
President & CEO, National Public Radio

SITEKE G. MWALE, Ph.D.
Executive Chairman, SGM Associates

CONSTANCE BERRY NEWMAN
Under Secretary, Smithsonian Institution

JAMES G. PARKEL

BARBARA REYNOLDS
Columnist/Editor, USA Today

PATRICIA B. SCALES, Ed.D.
President, Liberty Construction, Inc.

REV. YVONNE SEON-WOOD, Ph.D.

SCOTT M. SPANGLER
Private Investor

LOUIS W. SULLIVAN, M.D.
President, Morehouse School of Medicine

MARIA WALKER

.WALDENE E. WALKER, M.S., D.D.S.

CURTIN WINSOR, JR., Ph.D.
President, Legislative Studies Institute

President:
C. PAYNE LUCAS

Africare House, 440 R Street, N.W., Washington, D.C. 20001
Telephone: (202) 462-3614 • Fax: (202) 387-1034 • Telex: 64239

January 13, 1995

Mr. Rodney S. Penn
The Operational Unity Network
Houston, Texas
C/O SHAPE Community Center
3903 Almeda
Houston, Texas 77004

Dear Mr. Penn:

The purpose of this letter is to acknowledge
receipt of your very generous contribution in the
form of a check for $6,467.18 for our Rwanda
Relief program and to express our sincere
gratitude to the Houston Operational Unity Network
for the tremendous coordination effort in making
it all possible.

To date Rwanda relief activities include support
to 300 orphans; vegetable seeds and tools for
7,000 families; freight for shoes, clothing, and
food; medical care and medicines for four rural
clinics and support for medical personnel; and
restoration of safe water supplies. Your
contribution along with that of many other donors
will allow us to continue and to expand support in
these areas.

On behalf of the people of Rwanda I extend to the
Houston Operational Unity Network deep
appreciation for the concern and good will shown
for the less fortunate in distant lands.

Sincerely,

C. Payne Lucas
President

Contributions to Africare through Operational Unity Network

Azania (South African) Forum

Guest: Strini Moodley A.Z.A.P.O.
Black Consciousness Movement 300 People

Ta-seti African Awakening Conference

200-300 people

S.H.A.P.E. Center Kwanzaa

300 – 400 people

Minister Farrakhan Speech

35,000 Black Men

Family Day Nation of Islam

Houston Astrodome 21,000 people

Press conference leading up to the Million Man March, Operational Unity Representatives seated; circa 1994.

African Holocaust Conference
Shrine of the Black Madonna 3 Days, 1200 people

Operational Unity Participants seated at the table; circa mid. 1990s.

Two bus loads from Houston attended Millions for Reparations Rally in Washington D.C.; Circa 2002, representing a wide cross section of community interest.

There have been many other small and large joint actions, activities, events, and support for one another. The community seeing the symbolic and practical unity built a strong momentum and force.

One of the key lessons from the organization of OU is that when the lines of communication were opened, many real or perceived issues were solved and or addressed. Simple things like organizations having activities on the same date because of no communication were eliminated through a community calendar. I will talk more about unforeseen benefits of the project in another section.

Critique

In terms of things that could have been done better in OU during my approximately two years as coordinator, there were several. One major point that we never addressed was sustaining a coordinator economically. This is a historic and contemporary challenge that is faced throughout our movement, having paid organizers. Looking back, it could have easily been dealt with by having some portion of the money-making events go to the OU coordinator. Money and trust are sensitive issues in our efforts at unity. So many times, authentic efforts don't include finances, so not to give the impression of false motives.

Another area of concern is the concept of unity overtaking the correct effort of principled critique of actions and positions. What I am saying is when you have functional unity sometimes it is more difficult to challenge one another.

For instance, if another supports something and your group does not, then it sometimes becomes difficult to challenge them when they do something incorrect or take a bad position. Trying to keep everything cool in the spirit of unity. This could have been taken care of because of the good communication with scheduled structure opportunities to ask questions of each other on issues. In OU, groups are similar but different some spiritually, politically, some were more moderate and some more radical.

Unforeseen Benefits of OU

Sometimes the best of planners, organizers, and visionaries cannot predict all outcomes of a given project. This is because as a people we are not static and robotic, rather we move off rhythm, spirit, energy, and creativity.

Though this should have been easily foreseen, the power of having five organizations coming together meant that doors were open in dealing with community issues that would have been more difficult for just one group. Case in point, the mega conglomerate Clear Channel came into Houston to purchase three Black programmed radio stations. OU had issues with this and easily got the attention of the top leadership of the company.

To a certain extent, they were pandering to us temporarily to get what they wanted. In critical analysis, we mishandled the situation with a bootlicking diversion (Black person) being thrown into the mix. While we had the presence of force, all were not completely committed to using it in a boycott or some other action. Figuratively speaking, we did not squeeze the trigger. A lesson learned for me. This ability to bring a collective to the table benefitted us in many different instances. Simple reasoning tells you five can be more powerful than one.

I spoke earlier about opening up the lines of communication. What this has done is started a practice which takes place even outside of OU and has been adopted by others doing worthwhile work in the community. It is a standard if you will to interface with each other. That has cut down on some of the back biting and negative gossip in certain segments. Also, outside of OU participants communicate and collaborate on different efforts. OU has acted in the capacity of conflict resolution for other groups. This was not the intent but, people came to us with issues.

I have seen younger organizers and activists articulate the principles of OU because they have seen on many occasions OU in their community.

Taking it to Another Level

In 2005, the Operational Unity Network in Houston was being coordinated by Reverend Fanon of the Shrine of the Black Madonna. Reverend Fanon's coordination lasted a few years on a less intense level than the initial launch of the project. However, the bonds of built during this process are still functional today and have had national impact.

In order to revitalize the project forward, several things need to take place: 1. The Coordinator should be paid a decent stipend to cover basic needs, 2. Existing groups must further increase their commitment and planning, and 3. The participating organizations should be increased to include some diversity, specifically more youth-led efforts. (This can be done incrementally and phased in). The OU concept must go to the neighborhood/street level.

Fine Points for Organizers

I firmly believe that when you are really committed to something, you can perform various tasks you didn't think you could. At the same time, certain attributes are unique to different people. Some people have a natural disposition as diplomats, some people are straight ahead warriors/soldiers, and some people have multiple characteristics.

Being a coordinator/facilitator means understanding certain types of personalities have certain leanings. The Coordinator needs to be able to see the big picture, subordinate his/her ego for a greater good. Also, he/she must be able to meditate disputes in a non-bias way and be a good listener. Furthermore, this person(s) needs to be able to notice fine nuances about people or groups, their likes, dislikes and so forth.

Afterword

Dedicated organizer, humble community servant, nation-builder, front-line freedom fighter, and lover of Black/African people. Kofi Taharka is both a historian and a visionary, carefully connecting the intricacies of our past to the promise of our future, while unwavering in integrity and principle.

He is a voice for those who do not have one and inspires a voice in those who have not found theirs. He organizes from the street corner to the clubhouse, the prison to the pulpit, uniting black/African people along the way. He reminds us that "We do not wait to be invited to the table, we set our own table", and he does his best to make sure everyone can eat.

I am proud to call him my mentor, confidant, and dear friend. Forward Ever, Backward Never!

- Folade Madzimoyo

Struggle, Service, Sacrifice!

Special Asante Sana (Gratitude) to:

The Sisters and Brothers of the Operational Unity Network in Houston.

National Black United Front - National and Local Chapter (NBUF) - The Brothers and Sisters that have supported this idea.

Ta-seti African Historical Society
Lorenzo Jelani Williams
Elizabeth Bolingo Collins
Jarvis Taha Butler

Shrine of the Black Madonna
Cardinal Olu Ufum
Bishop Ada Edwards
Rev. Fanon

Nation of Islam Muhammad Mosque #45
Minister Robert Muhammad

Haitian American Ministries
Mawiyah Duperval

S.H.A.P.E Community Center
Deloyd T. Parker

Dr. Conrad Worrill and Rev. Jew Don Boney

NBUF
Dr. Conrad Worrill and Reverend Jew Don Boney

Ta-Seti
Lorenzo Jelani Williams

Shrine of the Black Madonna
Bishop Olu Ufum

Nation of Islam (Dr. Abdul Haleem Muhammad formerly Robert Muhammad)

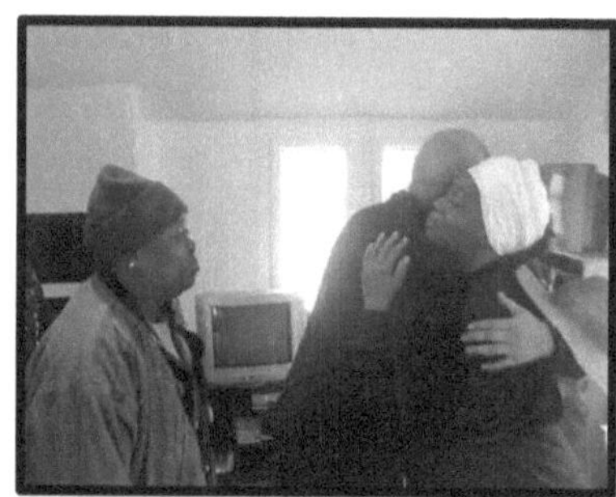

Haitian American Ministries (Mawiyah Buseje being welcomed back after earthquake in Ayiti, Haiti)

S.H.A.P.E. (Deloyd T. Parker Jr.)

NBUF is a formation consistently pushing practical unity in our communities.

Take a principled stand even when the odds appear to be against you.

Protesters shutdown Highway 288 in Houston, Texas over racial violence; TRAYVON MARTIN 2013.

NBUF members work in garden named in honor of Sundiata Acoli 2017.

www.ingramcontent.com/pod-product-compliance
Lightning Source LLC
Chambersburg PA
CBHW051426250726
48655CB00003B/1265